CHURCHILL'S SECRETARY
by
Linda Stoker

From the memoirs of her great aunt, Mary
Shearburn

Published by Beswick & Beswick Publishing House 2020
beswickandbeswick@gmail.com

BESWICK & BESWICK
PUBLISHING HOUSE

In memory of Mary Shearburn

With grateful thanks to Jacqui Stevens

and Andrew Searle

CONTENTS

Mary Shearburn

WORKING FOR WINSTON CHURCHILL

It seems strange now to recall I was not, at first, particularly impressed with the idea of working for Winston Churchill. Before the war, the ordinary man in the street hardly knew what to make of this out-of-office politician who, with repetition, issued solemn warnings of impending disaster. These were brushed aside by the leaders of his own party, who then ruled the country. To me, he was just another politician, and I imagined if I worked for him, I should need to have an interest in, and knowledge of politics.

I was without a job when the offer came. The one-man firm I worked for had ceased to exist after the owner's sudden death. Then I had an operation, and I was convalescing at the home of my sister, Kit, when a letter arrived from a secretarial agency in the City of London. It told me Mr Winston Spencer Churchill, MP, needed an extra secretary. The work would consist, of dealing with correspondence sent to him as Member of Parliament for Woodford, Essex and typing the manuscript of the book he was writing, 'The History of the English-Speaking Peoples'. I showed Kit the letter and told her I was not really interested. She, on the other hand, seemed to think it might be a worthwhile job. She persuaded me to do what the letter suggested - make an appointment with Mrs Hill, who had been Churchill's secretary for three years, and needed someone to help her with the work.

A few days later, I went along to a flat on the top floor of Morpeth Mansions, an apartment house in the London district of Victoria. Here, only a few minutes from the House of Commons, was Churchill's London residence. I met Mrs Hill, and I found her line of questioning a little

1

strange. After satisfying herself about my stenographic skills, she seemed unconcerned about my previous experience but quite anxious to know if I was engaged to be married - or likely to become so in the foreseeable future. I told her I had been engaged some years earlier, at the age of 20, and my fiancé died of tuberculosis. Since then, I had not considered marriage. This answer seemed to reassure, Mrs Hill and she asked me to call again the following evening to arrange an interview with Mr Churchill.

As I approached Morpeth Mansions for the second time, I still had no enthusiasm about working for the MP for Woodford. But it took only a few minutes of his famous charm to make me decide to give the job a trial. I was shown into the empty dining room. The door hardly closed before it reopened, and Winston Churchill, a portly figure, wearing black coat and striped trousers, walked towards me. He bowed slightly and held out his hand.

Almost in a fatherly way, he inquired about my schooling, my parents, and my general upbringing. He asked no questions about my efficiency, but no doubt Mrs Hill had already told him my shorthand speed was 140 words per minute and my typing 70. In fact, the only direct questions he asked about my proposed employment, was whether I minded working at night. I assured him I preferred the evening hours to the morning, explaining I was once a secretary to a theatre manager, where my work seldom finished before 11.30 pm. He gave a wry smile, held out his hand, and said, "Well, come to me for a month's trial. We'll see how we like each other."

LONG HOURS

Long before the month was up, I knew the reason Mr Churchill smiled - and why Mrs Hill was concerned about my marital prospects. His working day often went on until 2.30 am or later. No husband or fiancé would have tolerated those hours.

I arrived at Chartwell Manor on a mild April evening in 1939. I am not much of a country-lover, nor am I given to great enthusiasm for architecture, but I warmed to the mellow, red-brick house behind its semi-circular drive. A manservant in a short coat of white linen, opened the door and showed me to the office where Mrs Hill was sitting behind her desk. The office was a long, airy room, facing the front garden. Two desks stood inside a deep windowed embrasure. One was to be mine and I had pleasant visions of sitting by the open window during the summer months, looking out across the green sweep of lawn to the stately trees beyond. One wall of the room was covered in pigeon-holes, housing the galley proofs of the current volumes of 'The History of the English-Speaking Peoples'. Another wall lined with reference books and a third contained a fireplace where I never saw a fire - for we were to leave Chartwell when war began the following September. A large table in the middle of the room lay under a deluge of letters - some opened and some not. Many were from constituents, the kind of letters I could deal with in standard ways. Without reference to Churchill, I could pass them on to the relevant Government department or send a formal acknowledgement. An enormous backlog had accumulated, and Mrs Hill explained this was one of the reasons she needed an extra secretary.

CHARTWELL

Mrs Hill then showed me to my bedroom. I was enchanted. On the top floor, it gave me a magnificent view of the grounds through double aspect windows. The bedcover, chair, cushions, and the frill on the kidney-shaped dressing table were all patterned chintz. Matching curtains swayed by the open windows.

I unpacked and went down to the basement for dinner. I opened the door to find a pleasant sitting-room set aside for Mrs Hill and myself. During this first meal, I learned Churchill was dining also. When he had finished, his evening session of dictation would begin. His plan was to dictate to one of us for half-an-hour, then to the other while the first typed her notes in the office. We would take turns until he felt he had done a day's stint.

The plan seemed unnecessary and toilsome. I now learned we were to work six days a week, commencing at 9 am each day and remaining on duty until the late hour Mr Churchill decided to call it a day. True, there was a break of an hour or so in the afternoon, during which time Churchill would exercise his fantastic gift of laying his head down and falling asleep in an instant. Unfortunately, it was a trait I did not share.

When I told Mrs Hill of my difficulty in sleeping, she advised me to go to bed in the afternoons with a hot water bottle. I tried; but I succeeded only in making myself drowsy by the time I was due back in the office. I found it better to go for a brisk walk in the afternoon.

MY NOISELESS TYPEWRITER

Being a new broom, I tried a bit of sweeping. Why not, I suggested, take down the dictation straight on to a noiseless typewriter? Then, with no pause for transcribing notes, only one of us need be on duty each evening. But Mrs Hill told me my brilliant idea had already been put to Churchill. He had rejected it, convinced even the slightest sound would break his train of thought.

After dinner, Mrs Hill and I were in the office, struggling to reduce the mountain of letters, when a bell rang. It was the signal Churchill was ready to dictate. Mrs Hill suggested I should take the first session. She showed me up to the study.

Churchill was seated at his desk by an open window. He gave me a brief glance over the top of his reading spectacles, then waved his hand at a low armchair beside him. For a long time, he was occupied and silent. I took stock of the study. It was altogether delightful. A long room with high rafters. One wall had a sloping shelf, on which lay open books of reference. There was a huge brick fireplace, always laid out ready for lighting. The time was to come when my heart would sink as I watched Churchill amble across to this fireplace at midnight and put a match to the paper, sticks and coals - a sure sign of a long session to come.

I was still admiring the room when Churchill rose from his desk and began pacing the length of it. He was speaking in low tones, and panic-stricken. I strained to catch the words so I could take them down. It took me some minutes to realise the dictation had not yet started. Mrs Hill had forgotten to warn me of this constant habit of rehearsing in muttered undertones, making sure he had the exact words, before beginning to declaim them loud and clear.

After half-an-hour, the session came to an end. Before I left to transcribe the notes, he sat at the desk to sign some letters I had brought up. As he blotted the first signature, he held out a hand and barked,"Klop."

I stood bewildered. He turned to me, and I saw a mischievous glint in his eye. He pointed to a paper punch laying near my end of the desk.

"When I say 'Klop' Miss Shearburn, I mean I want you to hand me that." As he spoke, the telephone rang.

"Answer that please," he said.

I looked around but I could not see a telephone anywhere.

"Answer it, answer it," he said, as the ringing persisted. Again, I saw the gleam in his eye. I stood up and followed the sound until eventually, to my relief, I found the telephone nestling in a small alcove at the far end of the room.

Perhaps he was venting a little of his puckish humour to put me at my ease. Or, he was testing me, to see if I could think fast and act on my own initiative.

The first piece of initiative I showed was to persist in urging Mrs Hill to bring up once more the question of using a noiseless typewriter. After some pestering, Churchill agreed to give it a try. At first, he grumbled at the crackling sound as the paper fed into the machine. Then he began dictating. As the first page was complete, he lumbered forward, saying, "Gimme." He was delighted at being able to see the result of his work so fast. From then on, the noiseless typewriter was 'in'. Indeed, they were everywhere, there was one in his bedroom, and we had a special box made to take one on journeys. Among his family and friends, he presented the idea as his own. "Look," he told them, happy as a boy with a new toy. "I

6

can say 'Gimme' and I don't have to wait." Luxuriating in the occasional evening off, Mrs Hill and I were happy to let him take the credit. But we had to grow adept at whipping in fresh sheets for if his dictation were in full flow, he would never stop for anything.

My first weeks at Chartwell passed pleasantly as I found my way around. I grew to love the rambling old house with its warm, wood-panelled rooms and the curved staircase of polished oak.

I learned how to work a full day after only five hours' sleep and I began to enjoy my afternoon walk in the grounds, or through the surrounding countryside.

Mr Churchill discovered my spelling was not as accurate as his. I realised it was no use asking him for the correct spelling, for he would only say, "You ought to know." In later years he announced to assembled Chiefs of Staff, "If there are two ways of spelling a word, Miss Shearburn will invariably choose the wrong one." And the dear Generals and Air Marshalls would give me a sympathetic grin.

I earned my first rebuke after only a few days at Chartwell. We were at work on a volume of the 'History' which dealt with America, and he spoke of the States' intention to secede. I'd never heard of the word, but he refused my request for the correct spelling. "Seceed" I wrote. He firmly crossed it out, wrote in the correction and gave it back for re-typing.

On other occasions he could pick a phrase from the air which acted as a tonic. One night, before I grew accustomed to the long hours, we worked particularly late, and I must have shown my weariness. As he said goodnight, he looked at me and demanded, "You're not tired, are you?" I denied this terrible charge. He said, "No, you wouldn't be. You're a soldier's daughter."

When my month's trial came to an end, nothing was mentioned about whether my service should be required any longer. One night I mentioned this to Churchill. He seemed surprised. Then he smiled, gave me a slight bow, and said: "I am quite satisfied, Miss Shearburn. Are you?" I told him I was. And, in spite of the tedious, long hours, I took pride in my job. Part of this arose from my realisation of the importance of the work. Again, I took endless pleasure in his superb command of the English language - his gift for choosing words and making them 'sing on the page'.

Later, when he was Prime Minister, I saw his love of words lead him to a scathing comment, making my heart bleed for the person at the receiving end. Just before Italy decided to join in the war on the German side, Churchill made a strong attempt to dissuade the Italian dictator with a most eloquent letter referring to the 'river of blood' flowing between our two countries. He dictated the letter as I typed, then took the typescript and handed it to Sir Edward Bridges, son of a former Poet Laureate of England, who was secretary to the war cabinet.

Sir Edward read the Prime Minister's literary effort and handed it back with the words: "Jolly, Sir. Jolly." Churchill glowered at him and said: "Jolly. And you the son of a Poet Laureate." In my embarrassment I could have crawled through the keyhole. Sir Edward took the remark with great aplomb, making no effort to excuse himself, or to argue, or even to explain his curious choice of word.

***

If Churchill thought of an apt expression, a big grin would spread across his face. One evening, when he was First Lord of the Admiralty, I watched him reading a long document. His grin widened as he made a brief note in the

8

margin by the last paragraph. Outside, I mentioned this to the official secretary as I handed over the document, and we sneaked a glance at the paper to see what had so amused the Old Man. *(see note 1.)* We found the document contained a long-winded, sensational account, written by a Scottish official, involving a small boat putting to sea for the rescue of people from a sunken ship. The description was

excessively florid for what was, in the context of a world war, a small and routine incident.

At the end of the narrative, Churchill had written, 'Come the dawn'.

These amusements quite overcame my frequent irritation of his faults. He could, for instance, be extremely insensitive to the feelings and needs of others. He would work right up to the last minute before a mealtime, then bustle away, saying over his shoulder, "Have a fair copy of that ready for me immediately after lunch, will you?" He never considered secretaries must eat.

He liked to say, "There is no such word as 'can't,'" and by taking this attitude he tended to put his subordinates on their mettle. He got results, when a sympathetic word from him might have given someone an excuse to do nothing. His genius for not recognising other people's difficulties, was impressed on me during my first weeks in his employ. He wrote a fortnightly article for the British newspaper the *Daily Telegraph*, and these articles were simultaneously published in a French newspaper. For reasons of topicality, he seldom dictated them until the last possible moment. Often, there was so little time left, the manuscript had to be put on a passenger train for London, with arrangements made to have it collected on arrival. It was then too late to post the carbon copy to Paris. The solution, I was told, dictate the writings over the telephone to the Paris newspaper. I found it a terrible task to read 2,000 words over a bad line to a secretary whose understanding of English was almost nil.

CHURCHILL'S HATES

Some of his aversions seemed quite petty. He loathed the smell of Virginian tobacco, to such an extent, he forbade anybody to smoke it in his presence. It never seemed to occur to him, the smell of his cigars, infinitely more pungent than a pipe or cigarettes, might upset or annoy other people.

Soon after my arrival, I was warned about this idiosyncrasy, but nobody told me how keen his sense of smell was. One evening during the summer, whilst working alone in the office, I was smoking a cigarette and the door opened. In walked Churchill. It was unusual for him to visit the office. I slipped my stub in an ashtray and made sure the typewriter was between it and my visitor.

He wrinkled his nose.

"What," he demanded, "is that horrible smell?"

My mind whirred for an answer. Opposite the open window, foresters were burning the gorse over a large stretch of open woodland. I pointed to the rising smoke, suggesting this could be giving offense to his nostrils. His normal rebuke would have been, "If you must smoke cigarettes, use Turkish but don't smoke that horrible-smelling Virginian tobacco near me." On this occasion he said nothing, but I could see from his face, he was far from convinced by my explanation. No doubt he realised the office was my own ground. On the other hand, he admired quick-wittedness in others, so long as they did not lie to him, and I had not lied. Whatever the reason, I was spared the scathing comments.

On a later occasion, when he held his first wartime post as First Lord of Admiralty, he was not so considerate.

10

Dressed in what he called his 'rompers' (a zip-fastened one-piece overall of Air Force blue cloth) he strolled through my office at the Admiralty, puffing one of his huge cigars. I was smoking, and he complained about my 'obnoxious' cigarettes.

Without thinking, I pulled a rueful face. Glaring at me, he said, "Do not grimace when I speak to you Miss Shearburn." Crushed by the emphasis he had put on the word 'grimace', I was ever afterwards careful to control my facial expressions in his presence.

If he heard anyone whistling, Churchill would explode with wrath. During the war, a building known as the Annexe was being converted for our use and the builders often whistled as they worked. However faint the sound, the Old Man always heard it, and he would send someone out with the order, "Find out who is making that noise and tell him to stop at once." The job usually fell to Inspector 'Tommy' Thompson but on one occasion Tommy was absent. It was a quiet, sunny Sunday morning. I was working with Churchill on a high floor of Admiralty House when the silence was pierced by the sound of whistling outside the window.

Churchill peered at me over the top of his reading glasses and grumbled, "Open the window and tell him to stop that noise."

I went to the window, opened it, and looked out. Far below, an inoffensive civilian was crossing Horse guards Parade, whistling his joy at the sunshine.

"Go on," Churchill said. "Call out. Tell him to stop."

I thought the First Lord was going too far this time, and I said so. "The man is on a public highway," I protested. "He has every right to whistle." To soften the blow, I added, "He will be gone in a minute anyway."

To my relief and surprise, Churchill accepted this. Perhaps it struck him, the right to whistle in the sunshine was one of the smaller freedoms he was fighting for. Part of his unfeeling attitude to the foibles of others came from his determination to keep driving ahead at whatever job he had in hand.

CONCENTRATION

Churchill would become so absorbed in his work; nothing would distract him. For example, if he were perusing a paper when I entered and said, "Good morning," he would not reply. Perhaps 15 minutes later, the last paper dealt with, he would look up and say, "Good morning Miss Shearburn." He would allow nothing to interrupt his concentration.

BATS

Bats abound in the countryside around Chartwell, and on one hot evening, as I took dictation from Churchill in his study, a bat flew in the open window. Two things on this earth fill me with unreasonable terror, big, furry moths, and bats. With one of my mortal enemies about to dig its claws into my hair at any moment, I found it impossible to concentrate on shorthand. Churchill noticed my lack of attention and demanded an explanation. I told him about the bat. He was astonished such a thing should worry me, but he said with a grin, "I will protect you. Get on with your work." But he made no move against the bat and dismissed the creature's presence from his mind. I suffered agonies until I could escape the office. In spite of the heat, I kept the windows tight shut until I could leave.

WINSTON'S INTEGRITY

One other facet of Winston Churchill's character impressed me in those early days: his personal integrity, even in the smallest matters. This was brought home by a small but significant incident during that pre-war summer at Chartwell.

Among my personal belongings, I owned a copper, electric kettle. I kept it in my bedroom for making hot drinks and filling hot-water bottles. One evening, I found it burned out. One of the maids had, by accident switched it on, when dusting and left it to boil dry. It upset me, for it was an attractive kettle. Mrs Hill said, "Not to worry - everything in the house is covered by insurance." She sent in a claim, and in due course a cheque came to pay for the kettle's replacement.

That evening, among a batch of letters for signature, I presented the cheque to Churchill for him to endorse, before we sent it to the bank. He asked me what it was for, and when I told him, he looked grave. "But I am not insured for your possessions, Miss Shearburn. It would not be honest to take that money. Send it back. Tell them a mistake has been made. Your loss was due to the carelessness of one of my domestic staff, and the responsibility is, therefore, mine. I shall make good your loss."

CLEMENTINE CHURCHILL

I first met Mrs Churchill the day after I arrived at Chartwell, and I was struck by her attractive appearance and friendliness. The office telephone rang and Mrs Hill, told me Mrs Churchill would like some help with her

13

correspondence. I went up to her sitting room, a small but light and airy place, at the front of the house, furnished sparsely enough to allow plenty of room for movement. Later, I found this effect of spaciousness was typical of Mrs Churchill's style. It was evident in her bedroom, a large room with little furniture other than the bed, a big wardrobe, a dressing table, and several chairs.

Mrs Churchill wore tan slacks and a matching shirt, an outfit she favoured for days at home working in the house and garden. She greeted me with a friendly smile and handshake. I spent half-an-hour making notes on how she wished me to answer her letters, most of which were about clothes or invitations from friends. When we finished, she slipped on a pair of gardening gloves, took up a basket and a pair of pruning shears from a table. She went into the garden and began to cut a bunch of roses for the house. I often caught sight of her in her favourite rose patch, pruning the mass of blooms growing there.

I was fascinated by her clothes. In summer, the slacks and shirt were replaced by plain-cut linen dresses, whenever she left the house and grounds. In the evenings she wore long chiffon gowns in pastel shades which set off her snow-white hair. Later, in wartime her apparel became more sombre. But even during heavy air-raids in her Air Force Blue one-piece suit, modelled on Winston's 'rompers', she managed to look distinguished and sophisticated. Mrs Churchill took great interest in her clothes, and especially in her shoes. I was intrigued to find at Chartwell, in the corridor between her bedroom and her husband's study, a long, low cupboard housing dozens of pairs of her shoes. I found her fastidiousness excessive. If she lay down on her bed to rest during the day, a fresh pillowslip had to be fitted before she would retire for the night. When shopping, if she received her change in coins, she took them with a gloved hand and put them into a separate purse in her handbag. Arriving home, she gave the coins to a maid to wash them.

In the early months at Chartwell, I did not in the least mind helping Mrs Churchill. When war came, however, she took on innumerable tasks. Working for two busy people became almost impossible. I found myself doing Mrs Churchill's work during the mornings, and this often meant I must sacrifice my free time typing her letters in the evenings. One evening, Mr Churchill sent for me, only to discover my absence. I was still working for Mrs Churchill in the Admiralty House flat, and the First Lord had to wait while a messenger fetched me. He was irate and demanded an explanation. When he heard where I had been, he said no more; but within a week Mrs Churchill had her own secretary. This pleased me, not only because my life would be easier but also because just prior to this, Mrs Churchill had caused me trouble when she tried to find a paper of hers. I had filed it in the right place, but she did not understand the filing system, and scolded me for not being available to help her.

Apart from this one disagreeable incident, Mrs Churchill had shown kindness towards me. Once, when my bedroom was destroyed by bombing, she gave me a present of a beautiful black suede handbag. When I opened it, I found a cheque and a note telling me to use the money to replace some of the belongings I had lost. Another time, when I caught measles, she made many fruitless telephone calls trying to get me into a nursing home; but none would take an infectious case. In the end, she found me a private room in Fulham Fever Hospital. She sent me off there with a beautiful potted plant to brighten the place up.

Though she had a good memory, Mrs Churchill developed a unique way of making sure nothing was overlooked. At every conceivable point in her bedroom and sitting room, she left small, scribbling blocks lying about. Whenever she thought of something needing attention, she would make a note on a pad. Her secretary's first duty each morning was to gather the top leaf of each pad, then help Mrs Churchill decipher what she had written down - for her colourful handwriting was not particularly legible.

THE CHURCHILL FAMILY

Churchill was very fond of his family, especially his grandchildren. One of these children, Julian Sandys, seemed to inherit two of his grandfather's characteristics, his sense of mischief and his ability to face hard knocks. One day, when Julian was four, he kept tipping the contents of my office wastepaper basket on the floor. Tired of this game, I asked him to stop. He gave me a defiant look, deliberately emptied the basket again, and scooted through the door. This annoyed me, but my feelings changed to sympathy and admiration later in the day. In his bath he was equally defiant when his nannie told him to stop turning on the hot tap. She had to leave him for a moment, and he turned the tap on again, severely scalding his feet and ankles. He was confined to his bed for some days; but when I visited him, the child denied his pain.

Churchill was greatly concerned about the accident, and I know he was proud of the boy. I grew fond of Master Sandys over the years.

Randolph's son, Winston was born at Chequers in 1940 when I was working there during the war. It delighted Churchill when people said his baby grandson resembled him, though he was fond of saying, "If you stick a cigar into the mouth of any baby, it will look like me."

1939 AND WAR

Many people in Britain spent their last peace-time summer assuring each other there would be no war. Winston Churchill was not one of these. He could see war was the inevitable end of Hitler's policies. In the evening during dictation sessions, he would often break off and ask me to telephone the newspaper and ask what news was coming over the agency wires. In July 1939, the nation heard of the terrible disaster to the submarine *Thetis*, sunk with all hands off the coast of Britain. As Churchill worked on a speech he intended to make in his constituency, I learned all hope for the submarine crew had been abandoned.

For some time, Churchill sat in silence, staring at his desk. He turned to me, his face grave. "We'll have to scrap this speech, Miss Shearburn. I must re-write it."

It was a dark, blustery night, and through the windows I could see shadowy branches swaying. In sombre tones Churchill described the disaster and pictured the plight of the doomed mariners. His words so moved me, when he ordered, "Read that back," I could hardly control my voice. During my employment, I was to become the first to hear many of his speeches, which later became world-famous. Perhaps because it was the first time, I became aware of his great power over words, the speech in which he mourned the lost sailors of the *Thetis,* is the one remaining uppermost in my memory.

FRANCE

Soon after this incident, Mrs Hill told me, Mr And Mrs Churchill, together with Mary, their youngest daughter, were taking a holiday at the great country house, Chateau

St. Georges Motel in Normandy. It belonged to a relative, Madame Balsan. Mrs Hill explained she would be away on her own annual holiday at the same time, so I should have to go with the family to France - for even on holiday Winston Churchill had work for a secretary. I heard the news with trepidation. Up to then, I had always had Mrs Hill to lean on, and I was nervous of tackling the job on my own.

Still, there it was. Mrs Hill began initiating me into the performance needed to change the headquarters for the Old Man. I had to take along what amounted to a portable office. This included, assorted writing paper and envelopes, special pens, scissors, and glue. The famous 'Klop' had to go too, along with a box of green string tabs with brass ends. These were the only devices he would allow for fastening sheets of paper together, for it was one of Churchill's peculiarities. The thought of pins or paper clips drove him into an unreasoning fury, and Mrs Hill and I were always careful to remove any coming in the morning mail before he saw them. A copy of 'Vacher's Parliamentary Companion', a small booklet listing the names and addresses of members of the House of Commons and House of Lords and other information indispensable to Parliamentary business, all had to be packed. Winston's painting paraphernalia had to come too. And of course, his black silk band to put over his eyes in case he wanted to snatch one of his quick naps during the journey.

From Victoria Station, we travelled on the Blue Train, remaining in sleeping compartments throughout the Channel crossing and across the French countryside to Paris. Then, while Mary and her mother continued by train, Churchill and I travelled to Normandy by car. I saw little of the view, as I had to concentrate on the notes he was dictating. But at one moment he paused, and I noticed him gazing out over fields of corn, laying heavy and golden in the sunshine.

He shook his head, and he murmured, "Before this harvest is gathered in, we shall be at war." His words rocked me. Like everyone else, I had heard rumours of war. These had lessened a year earlier when Neville Chamberlain, the Prime Minister, returned to England from a visit to Hitler and waved a piece of paper at the newsreel cameras, promising, "Peace in our time". In my short months in Churchill's employ I learned, on the big, serious issues, he was seldom wrong. If he said war loomed, it undoubtedly was. His chilling words stayed in my mind through the long, hot days of our stay at the Chateau. They were days hanging still, under the summer's heat, and it seemed the whole world waited for his prophecy to be fulfilled.

At the Chateau, Churchill worked during the early mornings, then set up his easel in the grounds and painted. Much of my time I spent waiting in case he needed me. The holiday was supposed to end with a visit to the Duke of Windsor, the ex-King who had abdicated three years before. A sultry August dragged on. War came closer, and I was not really surprised, when one morning, Churchill rushed into my room and told me we should be returning to England at once *(see note 2.)*, but first I should come to his bedroom for some dictation. He sat up in his bed at the Chateau and looked out of the window. He spoke some words, which later impacted on my personal life - though neither of us could have known it. "Send a telegram," he said, "to Sergeant Thompson, asking him to meet me at Croydon aerodrome the day after tomorrow."

Sergeant Thompson. I made a note of the name. I had not the remotest idea of who he was at that time, or where to find him - but I knew better than to ask the boss before I tried every other conceivable way of finding out.

19

In Mrs Hill's absence, a former Churchill secretary, Mrs Pearman, had agreed to look after the office at Chartwell. I rang her and asked if she could throw light on the cryptic message. She explained, "Sergeant Thompson" was the Scotland Yard police officer who for many years had accompanied Winston Churchill as his personal bodyguard. Years before he had been promoted to the rank of Inspector, but the Old Man frequently forgot this detail.

"Leave it to me," Mrs Pearman said. "I'll send the telegram from here."

And I forgot all about 'Sergeant' Thompson until, a few days later, a tall, thin-faced stranger walked into my office and asked me for a gun.

Although Churchill would be flying back soon, I learned I was to follow by train, in company with Mrs Churchill's maid, Minnie. "You can bring the luggage," the boss said, with a lordly disregard of the problems I would likely encounter, while handling 17 pieces of luggage in a country whose language I did not speak. I will never know whether he was just being thoughtless or acting out of a misplaced regard for my capabilities. With Minnie, I boarded the local train, after discovering we should have to change for Paris. As so often happens when you are given directions in a foreign tongue, I was unsure of the name of the station where we had to change. We stopped at a place sounding about right, and I told Minnie to guard the cases while I made enquiries.

Leaning from the window, I tried to gain the interest of a solitary porter, but he doggedly looked the other way. I opened the door, stepped out onto the platform, and walked towards him. The train began to move.

I cried out in my appalling French and waved my arms. From the open window, Minnie emitted despairing cries. It was lucky, our obvious distress had the right effect on the French railway system. The train clanked to a halt,

20

and we got Churchill's luggage out and caught the Paris connection.

My Future Husband

The first time I met my future husband, he asked me to give him a revolver, and I said, "No." The gun lay in a drawer in my desk, at Chartwell. Churchill was back from an interrupted holiday in Normandy, and in another part of the house. It was August 1939 and war, imminent. Just a few days earlier Churchill had been warned by French Intelligence agents, Hitler had ordered his assassination. I had to be sure any weapon I handed out went to the right person.

He looked 'all right', this tall, long-striding man, who I had seen, from my window when he drove up in a long, black SS Jaguar coupé. His name, he said, Inspector Thompson. He was the very picture of a Scotland Yard Inspector, driving everybody's idea of a fast 1939 police car. I wanted to be careful - a Nazi assassin would hardly arrive wearing a brown shirt and singing the 'Horst Wessel' song.

I demanded he should identify himself. Quite unruffled by my suspicious manner, he began pulling bits of paper from his pockets, chose one, unfolded it and laid it on my desk. I read the telegram dictated by myself and sent to Inspector Thompson. Half-persuaded to hand over the gun, still, I held back. Daughter to a British Army major, I knew the potential danger of firearms in the wrong hands. I asked for more proof. This time the tall stranger tightened his lips a little and, without enthusiasm, dug once more into his pockets.

As he did so, it flashed into my mind there was an easy way to check this man's credentials. Inspector Thompson was well known to Winston Churchill, whose bodyguard

21

he had been over many years. Mr Churchill was in his study and from my office to the study - a direct telephone line.

But I did not lift the receiver. One thing I had learned, in the few weeks I had worked for Winston Churchill - you did not bother the Old Man with silly questions. He had a rare attribute that gives a great leader time to lead. He could delegate responsibility and expect people to go through fire and water to solve the problems he set.

So here, with nothing less than Winston Churchill's life in my hands, I had to take a decision. The tall stranger produced a Scotland Yard official driving licence made out to Detective Inspector Walter Henry Thompson of the Metropolitan Special Branch. It looked very authentic, and I decided to hesitate no longer. I opened a drawer of my desk and took out the revolver, Churchill's own Colt .45. I checked the safety catch and, making very sure it was pointing away from us both, handed it over.

As the Inspector went out, I felt a twinge of embarrassment. I wondered what he - a tried and trusted member of the Churchill establishment would think of a raw recruit like me, putting him through my one-woman version of a wide-mesh security screen. As it happened, I had no need to worry. At 2.30 am after what I and the other Churchill secretary, Mrs Kathleen Hill, called 'late work', I was putting away my typewriter when Inspector Thompson came in and asked if I would like a cup of tea. I accepted with pleasure. We talked for half an hour, Churchill's private secretary and Churchill's private detective, little realising it was the first in a long series of conversations and cups of tea. Six years and a world war later, we would marry.

AIR-RAID ON LONDON

Only a few days were to pass before war was declared, on September 3, 1939. Normal daily routine - cast aside. Mr and Mrs Churchill, Mrs Hill, and I, were continually dashing between Chartwell and the London flat in Morpeth Mansions. At last, we settled in London. Mrs Hill and I made up beds for ourselves on the floor of the dining room.

September 3 was a Sunday. Churchill instructed us to assemble in the drawing room just before eleven o'clock in the morning. As Big Ben tolled the fateful hour, the voice of Prime Minister, Neville Chamberlain declared over the radio, we were at war with Germany. Then came a chilling experience. Within seconds of the end of the broadcast we heard, for the first time, the air raid siren. It was a banshee wail of street alarms that would haunt our lives for the following five-and-a-half years. As it happened, this turned out to be a false alarm. A British aircraft had triggered the nervous hands of those in charge of the system, but we were not to know this until much later. Believing London, like Warsaw a few days before, was under heavy attack from the air, we trooped to the air raid shelter in the building's basement, led by Churchill. On his way out, he snatched up a bottle of brandy, preparing for a long siege. Once in the shelter, he made an impromptu speech to the people assembled there, telling them all to remain calm, and pointing out this was just what one might expect of Hitler, "that horrible man," and his "Nahzis" (he always refused to attempt the German pronunciation) – "an attack within minutes of the end of the ultimatum given by the British Government."

As luck would have it, for all of us, Churchill was wrong on that occasion. After a few minutes, the 'all clear'

23

sounded, and we returned to the flat. On hearing future alarms, Churchill instructed us, we were to take first aid equipment to the shelter, together with whisky, ice and soda water for him, and sherry for the ladies.

```
              Air Raid - 1940.
              -----------------


She was running - running to safety...
  The only safety she knew.
But the small feet couldn't run fast enough
  So she died.....by a shot from the blue.

By a shot that an enemy airman fired
  As the small figure ran for her life.
And only God in His Heaven knows
  Why a child should pay for our strife.

We made this war - and we suffer -
  That's only fair and right,
But that a child should get even a glimpse
  Of the terror that comes by night

Is a thing they'll pay for one of these days,
  If it costs us all we prize.
They'll have to pay for the terror that lay
  In a little dead child's eyes.

They deliberately maching-gunned a little child
  Who was running...she hardly knew why.
But the memory will haunt me all my days
  Of a little child running...to die.
```

Poem written in 1940 by Mary Shearburn after a traumatic experience of a child dying in an air raid.

BACK AT THE ADMIRALTY

Churchill's latest promotion was to First Lord of the Admiralty, "Much better than I expected, Miss Shearburn." A heartening message went out, to all the ships of the British Navy, 'Winston is back'. He took up his duties without delay. At the end of his first night's work, while we were returning to Morpeth Mansions in his car, he told me there would be a change in my position as his secretary. He would now, have official Admiralty staff, but if I cared to stay on, he would be pleased for me to do so. I would be paid by the civil service, but he would add a retaining fee to cover any work on his personal affairs. I was pleased to accept but I soon discovered, in spite of his having an official staff, there would be no lessening in my hours of work. In fact, they grew longer as the war went on. The staff, both at the Admiralty and later when he became Prime Minister at his official residence, 10 Downing Street, worked normal office hours. I was still largely responsible for the late work, except for one day each week when I was off duty for a full 24 hours.

FALLING FOR TOMMY

Inspector Thompson was never far from Churchill's side. Tommy, as I learned to call him, had no place of his own to wait, when the boss was safe in his Admiralty office. He needed to be at the nearest point to the man he was guarding. Other than sitting in a corridor, the closest place to Churchill was my office. He would often have to wait for hours, and soon we got into the habit of going to lunch together. He explained about his marriage, but for some years he and his wife had not got on well, having originally disagreed over the long and uncertain hours of his job as bodyguard to Winston Churchill. Tommy, was an extremely upright man, so never suggested our relationship was anything other, than two people thrown together by our work and being friends with one another.

I remember wondering how many other men would have behaved in such a correct manner as he did when, to get a breath of air, I accompanied him on his late-night security patrol in the deserted grounds of Chartwell. Still, there were tiny pointers to the future, though they have become apparent only in later years. For instance, on a cold winter's Saturday afternoon, I found myself shivering in the stands at a soccer match. The first I had ever attended in my life. We were cheering for Tommy's favourite team, Tottenham Hotspur. Afterwards, in a little café near the stadium, we enjoyed sausages and mashed potato, or 'bangers and mash' as they are called by football fans.

"Tommy" Thompson, Churchill's Scotland Yard Detective

When Winston gave me a grudging two hours off on Christmas Day, 1939, I took Tommy across to Notting Hill for a Christmas dinner cooked by my mother. A few days later, given two days off for working through Christmas, I went to Weston-Super-Mare, the Somerset resort where my sister, Kit lived. Tommy drove me there in his black Jaguar. After a telegram told Tommy, Churchill was leaving on a journey at midnight, there was a mad chase back through fog, eating ham sandwiches, prepared by Kit in a hurry.

WRITING SPEECHES

Churchill was a night person. He could always work better when the official working day was over. This was due to fewer interruptions. His facility for taking recuperative 'catnaps' at any hour of the day or night, helped to keep him fresh and alert. Whatever the reason, it was late at night, or in the small hours, when he wrote most of his famous speeches and framed important directives for sending to the Generals and Admirals in charge of war operations across the world.

Working on a Churchill speech was an exhausting but fascinating business. At first he dictated a rough draft - an easy job for me, because I could use a single sheet without the bother of changing carbons and 'flimsies', a task that always must be accomplished without the 'crackling', annoying him. In this first stage, I would be thrilled to see the story evolving under my fingers, with the certainty there would come one of those stirring passages, setting the world afire and lifting the hearts of men facing mortal danger.

I can still remember the original shaping of one of his most famous sentences, his glorious tribute to the air crews of the Royal Air Force, at the time when the Battle of Britain was at its height in the late summer of 1940. We were in the Cabinet room at 10, Downing Street, sat at the long table where Cabinet ministers gathered for their historic meetings. Churchill positioned himself half-way along one side of the table, his back to the big, open fireplace. I sat opposite him, quiet and waiting for him to lift his head from the documents he was reading.

He rose from his chair and walked up and down, dictating one of his long speeches on the progress of the war - to be delivered to Parliament the following day.

When he came to the paragraphs dealing with the war in the air, he muttered to himself for a while, seeking as he so often did, the exact words. My typewriter lay quiet. He stopped walking. He stood erect and still, and I was startled and moved to see tears running down his face. Still standing at attention, he declared those famous words which, a little later, I wrote out again in what he called his 'speech form' - broken into lines like blank verse, for easier reading:

> "Never in the field of human conflict
> Was so much owed
> By so many
> To so few."

***

In the eventful years following, I was to feel a whole range of emotions towards Winston Churchill - from fascination to fury. He could be light-hearted and talkative, silent, and irascible. He could be charming and amusing, or moody and boorish. The only thing I could be certain of, his total unpredictability. I never knew what I was expected to do next, or where I should have to go. And to make any difficulty about even his most outrageous demands, would court disaster. According to him, there was always a way. Those who worked for him, should find the way.

Only once do I remember being prepared for one of his swift changes of plan. Early in the war, before the German's invaded, he took me with him on a visit to France. Sometime later, he proposed another trip, but announced he would require secretarial assistance only as far as the channel port of Dover. Sure enough, as the train drew into Dover, he said he had not finished the work he intended doing, and I would have to go to France. I surprised him by remaining calm about this and I even told him the idea appealed to me very much.

He raised his eyebrows: "What will you do about clothes and so on?"

I revealed my secret. Suspecting I might have to cross the Channel, I packed a case and there it was, up on the luggage rack.

He gave me a look that was hard to interpret. I took it, rightly or wrongly, to mean, "You're learning fast, my girl."

FRANCE AGAIN

My first wartime trip to France made history in a way. Women never went to sea in warships, especially in wartime. But the First Lord of the Admiralty crossed the Channel in the destroyer *Codrington*, and as the First Lord's personal secretary, so did I. As we went aboard, the officers were lined up to greet Churchill. I was introduced to them, and one officer instructed to look after me. This officer, knew my naval officer brother, having served with him on another ship.

They royally entertained me, and I was shown around the ship. On the bridge, I became intrigued by the ASDIC equipment - the device for sending out sound waves which, reflected by a foreign body, could indicate the presence of enemy submarines. I asked how it worked - then remembering the wartime need for secrecy, I added with haste, "That is, if it's all right to tell me, of course." The officers laughed. "Surely," one said, "we are allowed to tell the First Lord's secretary anything she wishes to know."

Tommy, who was there to guard the boss, became a little chilly towards me for much of this trip. At one point in the tour, the officers invited me into the wardroom. We were all drinking and talking when I caught sight of Tommy standing in the doorway. He wore a black expression.

"Ah," I thought.

Churchill, I know, was secretly hoping to see some action while at sea, and he would have loved it if the ASDIC had picked up a U-boat. However, he was told the sounds it was picking up, were being bounced off nothing more dangerous than the coast of France. Not to be frustrated, he spotted some floating mines, and asked for them to be blown up. Normal routine would be to leave them alone for the minesweepers to deal with. But he was the First Lord and he got his bangs.

On landing in France, there was a short walk from the ship to the Paris train. Members of the party carried the official boxes, and Churchill gave one of them to me. Already loaded with my own case, I struggled along when Lord Halifax courteously took the heavy wooden box, saying, "That's no job for a woman." Sometime afterwards, I learned he had a withered arm and carrying the box was no simple task for him.

We stayed overnight in Paris, I at the Hotel Crillon, the rest of the party at the British Embassy. I was looking forward, with excitement to the following day, when I expected to be one of the few women to visit the front lines. When I arrived at the Embassy the next morning, however, Churchill told me it had been decided, the journey would be difficult and unsuitable for a woman. He saw the disappointment on my face, and said he was sorry, but it could not be helped. Strange how he would never notice if I had been overloaded with work or luggage, yet he would sympathise if I were to be denied the chance of an adventure. It was something of the attitude one expects from a young boy towards a tomboy girl.

In this instance, my disappointment was short-lived. The following day Tommy telephoned to say the First Lord wanted me for some work. I was to make my way to Arras immediately. Again, the Churchillian disregard of other people's difficulties. He must have known a foreigner could not travel at will through a country at war - with the enemy poised all around its borders. But as usual, he simply gave an order and expected me to find a way to carry it out. I could not just go and buy a railway ticket to Arras. I did what seemed to be the obvious thing. I went to the Naval Attaché at the Embassy, the natural person to help the First Lord's secretary. He flat-out refused my request. "Out of the question," he said. "Nobody, particularly a civilian, and more especially a woman, could go roaming around the French countryside." Not for Churchill's secretary? I made it clear I was not going to accept his refusal, and at length he agreed to contact the Military Attaché. I went through the same procedure with them, beginning with a blank refusal. "Impossible." he said. I argued, when Winston Churchill wanted something done, nothing was impossible. He finally gave in, presented me with a 'safe conduct' docket and washed his hands of me.

Tommy met me at the station at Arras. He took me to Military Headquarters, where I soon found myself plunged into the familiar routine of taking dictation from the boss. Typical, Churchill never inquired whether I had found the journey difficult. He had given an order and I had obeyed. To him, it was the way of the world.

And there was more to come. The work only took a few hours. Then Churchill told me to return to Paris and take the official box containing the secret documents on which we had been working. Highly unusual, as such boxes were normally entrusted only to official messengers - men trained in the task of preventing valuable Government secrets from falling into the wrong hands. Churchill stressed the importance of the papers, and gave me, as bodyguard, a French officer. Neither of us could speak the other's language, so we travelled in cold, uncomfortable silence. Back at my hotel in Paris, I rang the office of my old friend, the Naval Attaché to ask him to arrange for the box to be collected. He had left for the night. Feeling I had the fate of nations in my feeble hands, I locked the box in my wardrobe, put the key under my pillow, and hardly dared sleep until it was delivered to the Embassy the following day.

OFFICIAL BOXES

This was not the only occasion I had to look after an official box. When the First Lord visited Scapa Flow, the great Naval base in the wilds of Scotland, he found his work unfinished. He told me I must go part-way with him, work on the train as far as Carlisle, then return with the box. He told me a sleeping compartment would be booked for me. I gathered this was for the safety of the box rather than for my comfort.

Stressing how important the papers should arrive without mishap, Churchill demanded, "What would you do, Miss Shearburn, if during the train journey you were to be attacked, and the safety of those papers threatened?"

"Scream," I said, "at the top of my voice, and at the same time kick my assailant's shins with all my might."

He looked amused. "I believe you would, and I believe it would work."

Thank goodness, nobody attempted to snatch the box. When I got off the train at Carlisle, the stationmaster met me. When the London train came, two huge policemen escorted me to my sleeping car. Anyone watching me, must have thought I had been arrested.

There was an uncomfortable day when an official box did get lost while in my charge. We spent a weekend at the country home of the Digby family, who were the parents of the first wife of Winston's son, Randolph. When the party returned to London, Tommy and I were told to look after a number of boxes, and a Treasury messenger had the job of seeing them onto the train. Tommy and I had to find seats in separate compartments. He took the boxes.

After the train got under way, Tommy came to see me and asked if I had a box with me, he had counted them and found one missing. Alarmed, I told him I did not have the box. Tommy pulled the communication cord. The train jolted to a grinding halt, and a guard appeared. We had gone too far for the train to be taken back to the station. But the guard arranged for us to wait at the next station and have the box - which still lay on the platform - sent on. Of course, Churchill demanded to know why the train had stopped, and when told the reason, he had Tommy 'on the carpet'. This was no isolated occurrence. When things went wrong, Tommy, who was usually on hand, got blamed by the Old Man, often when he had no part in the offence. On this occasion, Churchill suggested part of the blame must lie with me, but Tommy denied this and took everything on his own, broad shoulders. A few minutes later, Churchill sent for me. Not knowing what Tommy had said, I apologised 'for overlooking the box'. Though angry, Churchill seemed slightly mollified as we had both accepted responsibility and not tried to lay the blame elsewhere. He hated it when people would not admit their mistakes.

Though I was uncomfortable whenever I found myself in charge of these precious secrets, I was proud of the trust Churchill put in me. This faith was usually unspoken, but once Churchill did put it into words. He was then Prime Minster. My youngest brother came to see me after his ship, the *HMS Southwold*, had been sunk by enemy action and I introduced him to Churchill at the door of the Cabinet room. They talked for a few minutes and Churchill said to him, "Go along, take your sister out to lunch. I won't tell her not to talk about anything she should not mention, because I know she won't."

Of course, I was aware of countless Top-Secret matters, but these went into a mental pigeon-hole labelled 'work', and I never spoke of them. Even Mrs Hill and I never discussed anything which came in the Secret category. There was a routine for dealing with such papers. We handed all copies to Churchill the moment they were typed. Then we burnt the carbon papers. It was strange but we seemed to simultaneously burn the secret knowledge from our memories.

WARTIME WORKING ARRANGEMENTS

The coming of war meant the loss of my cosy bedroom at Chartwell, and the beginning of a series of strange and often uncomfortable sleeping places. Mrs Churchill's first suggestion was Mrs Hill and I should find lodgings in London, but with the hours we worked, it would have been almost impossible, and I did not relish walking home through the air raids at 3 am.

I looked over Admiralty House, and soon knew the layout of the place. On the top floor was a flat for the First Lord and his family. Below, down to ground level, were the offices, the official dining room, and other public rooms. In the basement, I found a number of rooms in various states of disrepair, and from an official of the Office of Works - the Government department responsible for official buildings - I learned it would be possible to turn two of these into bedrooms. Mrs Churchill gave her consent. They were far from palatial - and until the Office of Works renovated them, there were mice to keep us company. But, when the mice had been removed, the rooms were reasonably comfortable - and more important, handy for our work.

As I struggled to accustom myself to the strain of wartime working, I found myself relying more and more on the unobtrusive help given to me by Tommy. His long years with Churchill gave him an insight into the Old Man's ways, and he could often give me valuable advice when I was floundering. Mrs Hill started work earlier than I, as mine were the late-night shifts. Thus, she went to lunch at 12.30 am and I waited until she returned. By 1.30 pm Churchill was ready for his meal, so Tommy and I were usually free at the same time. Our evening meal breaks also coincided, and we fell into the habit of eating together in the Admiralty canteen. Again, if Churchill stayed up at night, Tommy had to be near. On journeys, he had to be within arm's length of Churchill. He made himself useful by helping me with the great mound of office equipment. This included a big, office typewriter, I had to take everywhere with me. Tommy often knew when the Old Man was about to take his half-hour afternoon nap, and he would warn me, in case I wanted to slip out for any reason.

Churchill seemed to work on the assumption I did not need any private time. But one thing we could all bank on - the Old Man missed nothing, though he might not always comment. After one weekend at Chequers, he marched into my room late on Sunday evening and announced we must return to London. I was the only secretary with him, and I travelled in his car. With drawn blinds, he dictated the draft of a forthcoming speech. When we arrived, I went straight to my office and started to transcribe the notes.

Close on midnight, his bell rang, and I went into his office for more dictation. For about quarter of an hour we worked. Then he said, "What about the notes you took in the car? Why doesn't someone else come to me now so that you can be working on those?" I explained there was nobody else about. He seemed annoyed.

"Go and wake Mrs Hill and tell her I want her," he growled. Having often being woken myself in this way, all my sympathies were with Mrs Hill. I told him as nobody knew we were returning during the night; Mrs Hill would probably not be in the building. "In any case," I said, "It will mean keeping you waiting while I go and see." It did the trick. He did not want to be kept hanging around. He permitted me to remain, but he was grumpy.

"You have nobody but yourself to blame if you have to stay up late and write out the other notes," he said. As usual, Churchill had the last word, but Mrs Hill got her rest.

Another time, when I was due to go on a journey with him, we worked until 3.30 am the previous night, and little time for sleep. At 8.30 am Tommy came along the train to my compartment, to say the Old Man wanted a secretary.

When I went into his compartment his eyes were down, reading, and he did not look up for a while. When he did so, he seemed astonished. "What, you again?" he asked. He seemed exasperated. "You were working until 3.30 am this morning. Can't some better arrangement be made, so whoever does the late work is not expected to be available early the following morning?"

I told him I did not want to miss the trip. I pointed out, he had been working until 3.30 am and here he was ready to start again. I thought I saw him smile, but the only answer he gave, was a grunt.

He became so engrossed in his gigantic task; Churchill often gave the people around him the feeling he was totally inhuman. But on occasions, before you had time to swallow your anger, he would, without warning, change his attitude.

I shall never forget one incident, right at the beginning of the war, when none of us knew just what dangers we were about to face. My sister intended taking her small daughter to live out of London - soon to become the bombers' main target. I knew she needed help with packing her furniture. I waited until, during a car journey, there was a moment when Churchill was doing no work. I asked him for a day off and explained the reason.

"No." he said. I was shocked by the fierceness of his tone. "This is not time to think of domestic matters. World events are shaping. The time will come when you will be proud to have lived in these momentous days." That evening, when he had finished a session of dictation, he turned to me. "You wanted to go and help your sister. You can take the day off tomorrow."

On another evening, after a long and busy day at the Admiralty, he said, "These are hard times Miss Shearburn, but I expect at the end of the war you will get a medal for your share." In fact, I did not get a medal - perhaps because illness forced me to leave his service before the Nazis were beaten. I did not particularly want one, and as he seemed in a relaxed humour, I told him so. "I would rather be allowed to go on more journeys with you." He smiled and said, "I think you probably would."

THE TRAVELLING SECRETARY

These trips made a welcome break from office routine. We worked hard enough, whether in cars, trains, or boats - less in boats because the First Lord of the Admiralty was not a particularly good sailor. I enjoyed the air of informality that never existed in London. There were difficulties, of course, such as trying to type in a tiny, swaying sleeping compartment, with the Old Man sitting up in bed. Sometimes a trip outside London, could bring home, with a vivid clarity, the events which to me, were simply words on paper.

One such journey was an exciting visit to Dover, the town in Britain, nearest to Europe. Below Dover Castle, carved deep in the cliffs, lay an enormous Defence Headquarters. Here and there, outlets through the cliff face gave a panoramic view of the English Channel, looking towards France – twenty-one miles away. On our way through the rocky HQ, our party stopped at one of these openings. I held my breath while we watched an aerial dogfight out over the sea. Our fighters brought down a German plane and I felt my heart thump in my chest. Churchill was delighted. As we left, Dover was shelled from France by German guns.

Later, from our cavalcade of cars, we saw a plane coming down in flames. My hands were shaking, and I could not take down any dictation. Churchill demanded to be driven to the crash. A look of relief swept over his face when he learned the plane was German. I watched in awe as the pilot floated down to earth, attached to his parachute. The local defence force were there to pick up the airman. For him, the war would be over.

This journey was full of incidents. We went on to Ramsgate, another 'front-line' town. The air-raid sirens sounded, and we were all hustled to a shelter inside a huge tunnel.

Churchill told me to put my steel helmet on. I was compelled to carry this protection equipment everywhere, strapped to my satchel containing the heavy service respirators. I found it cumbersome and among the greatest irks of the war. The rule - they were to be carried everywhere, on duty or off. This was no problem for

Churchill, as Tommy always carried the Old Man's in addition to his own. I rarely put the great heavy thing on my head - it ruined your hair. But an order from the First Lord had to be obeyed. As I slipped the strap under my chin, I was amused to see all the officers in the entourage uncomfortably following suit.

One man made me laugh as we entered the shelter. He was one of a group of workmen who stood at the entrance of the tunnel. Churchill, as always in public, smoked a big cigar. The workman, grinning, said, "No smoking inside." He held out his hand, and Churchill gave him the cigar. The man stayed outside the tunnel for the duration of the raid. He was still there, enjoying Churchill's cigar, when we came out at the 'all clear'.

I went many times with the First Lord on his visits to the fleet at Scapa Flow. Although, never allowed beyond Thurso, the nearby town on the Scottish mainland. The Naval-Officer-in-Charge and his staff were always wonderful and kind. Sometimes, they organised a dance with a band, especially for me. It was amusing and flattering to be treated as someone of great importance - such a contrast to my position in the office in London and I revelled in the reflected glory. Perhaps, in a perverse way, as I enjoyed it even more when a glance from Tommy showed me his displeasure at the attention I was getting from the Naval officers. We had never spoken of romance, but we were growing closer.

FINDING COMFORT

Tommy and I went out together whenever we could snatch a few hours off at the same time. We often went to an Inn, The Grafton, near Leicester Square, where the sherry was marvellous and, for a time, steaks were still on the menu. There was another restaurant near Victoria Station and a nearby cinema, which we sometimes visited. We went to one or two shows, *Black Velvet* with the star Vic Oliver, then married to Churchill's daughter Sarah. And the Noel Coward play, *Blythe Spirit*.

During our talks, Tommy gradually poured out his troubles. They all stemmed from his work guarding Winston Churchill over many years. Back in the 1920s his job had kept him away from home when he had to accompany Churchill on weekend visits, and even when they were in London, he often could not get home until 3 am. The resultant friction caused him to part from his wife and family of three boys and two girls. His work as Churchill's bodyguard had affected his financial situation too. For one thing, it cut across the strict Scotland Yard rules about promotion. As Churchill's bodyguard he was away from what the Yard considered his real job, as an officer of the Special Branch. Colleagues with less service passed him by. Even returning from civilian life to take up his wartime appointment had wrecked his finances. He had been doing well in business and was the owner of two grocery stores. The men working for him were called into the Services, and his job left him no time to look after the shops himself. He lost them both.

His family lived in Yorkshire. One day, with a tear in the corner of his eye, he showed me a letter he had received from his youngest daughter *(see note 3.)*. A sad little note which told of the other girls at school. Their daddies came home on leave. The unspoken message was, she did not have a daddy. This letter drew me up with a jerk. Though we had never spoken of marriage *(see note 4.)*, I realised we had dropped into a way of thinking, we might have a future together. I told Tommy he ought to try to patch up his marriage, and he agreed. He sent for his wife, and she came to London. But, apart from a few snatched visits for afternoon tea, he still could not find the time to be with her.

On one of these visits, she said to him: "It's no use, is it? I'm wasting my time staying here. You have no affection for me anymore. It's all gone." He told her about me, and she said "I don't think I'll stand in your way. I'm going to divorce you for desertion." They both agreed there was nothing left of their marriage.

There was never anything so formal as a proposal of marriage from Tommy to me. One thing holding Tommy back was the feeling he had, he would not survive the war because of Churchill's habit of continuing to walk into danger. But after this final break with his wife, we simply accepted, when the divorce came through, we should marry.

Inspector Thompson's sergeant, Cyril Davies and Mary Shearburn, 1941.

PRIME MINISTER

Winston Churchill became Prime Minister in 1940, elected by common consent of the Members of Parliament from all parties. We moved into 10, Downing Street, the 18th Century house, used as home and office by Prime Ministers in Britain. Churchill worked each day in the Cabinet room, sitting at the centre of the long table, with me opposite by my typewriter. Often, and especially at night, he wore his warm rompers, prepared if necessary, to work on in a cold air raid shelter. When he had a heap of official papers to read, time would crawl by as I sat motionless, waiting for my part to begin. Behind his head, on the mantelpiece, stood a large clock. It seemed to hypnotize me as I watched the hands crawling round. At other times, when he was dictating almost continuously, time would fly, and I would look up at the end to see it was 3 am.

One-night stays in my mind. Britain had been losing heavily in North Africa, and Churchill was troubled. As he ploughed through boxes of official papers, he stopped at times, shaking his bowed head from side to side and muttering to himself. He looked weary and I was tired. I dropped off to sleep. I woke suddenly as he banged shut the lid of one of the boxes. He came to his feet and looked at the clock. It was 1.30 am. He sighed and said, "It's early yet - we must press on."

He drove himself to the limits of his strength. As a result, those of us who worked under him, offered no complaint when he expected us to do the same. When the first Christmas of the war arrived, I expected the holiday would be recognised by a little relaxation but I was quickly put straight by Churchill when I asked, on Christmas Eve, what time he would require me the following morning, "Eight o'clock of course, as usual."

Perhaps some surprise showed on my face, for he then gave me a sharp glance and said: "Oh, did you want to go to church, Miss Shearburn?"

"No," I told him, "I just wondered whether we should be keeping normal working hours on Christmas Day."

In a soft voice he said, "Oh well, make it eight-thirty." Lord Halifax, who overhead this half-hour Christmas gift, was amused.

Moving to Downing Street meant a vast improvement in my sleeping accommodation. The private quarters at the top of the house were large enough to allow Mrs Hill and myself a bedroom each. I had a nice room overlooking a small, green at the side of the house, but my stay was a short one. Four months after we moved in, the heavy air raids began. One night, a bomb dropped on the nearby Treasury building. The same one had damaged No. 10, demolishing my bedroom.

We had been working at the Annexe in the evenings, during the heavy air raids. It was a bomb-proof building adjoining the Air Ministry, and that night we all slept there for safety. The following day Churchill went to No. 10, to inspect the damage. In my room, an enormous wooden rafter lay across my bed.

"You would have been alright, Miss Shearburn," he said. "The bed is still there." I was glad I had not been there to test the truth of his theory.

With my room gone, I slept permanently in the Annexe. The Churchills had a flat there, and bedrooms were also available for them in the basement, under a 15-foot thick concrete and steel covering. On the same basement level, Cabinet rooms and other offices ensured, no matter how noisy the war got at night, the work of directing operations could go on without interference.

Churchill hated sleeping in the basement and avoided it whenever he could. He never liked creeping into corners to avoid bombs. While the Annexe was being built, the Railway Executive came up with a brilliant plan to provide safe working quarters for the Prime Minister. In Down Street, Mayfair, just off Piccadilly, there was an old, disused Underground Railway station, where the Railway people, had built a set of offices 120-feet below ground.

It took a lot of persuasion to get the Old Man to go down there. He seemed to have a horror of being deep underground. He would rather see what was happening with the bombs. Inside the unobtrusive entrance there was a lift which took us part-way down. Then we had to descend several flights of stone steps to a lower level where the offices were. Down still more steps, there was a dining room and a row of small bedrooms, like compact little ship's cabins.

For a short time, Churchill endured working there and sleeping to the roar of passing trains. Each morning, at first light, he was off to No 10. There he worked sitting up in bed, wearing a quilted silk bed-jacket, until it was time to bath and dress for the day's first meeting - usually about 10 am. He was much happier when we moved into the Annexe. So was I. Descending each night into Down Street, meant carting a lot of office equipment across London, and I was terrified the night would come when Churchill would demand something I had not thought to bring.

A bomb fell near the Annexe before the strengthening of the ground floor structure was complete. The explosion shook the building and put out all the lights. I was working with a Treasury official in the small underground office. The official produced a torch, and by its light we saw Churchill lumbering through the door. "Miss Shearburn," he said, "we've been hit."

He began climbing the stairs towards ground level to investigate the damage. General Ismay and Tommy went with him and I began to follow.

Churchill turned and saw me.

"Go back to your rabbit warren," he demanded.

I saw a grin on Tommy's face. Churchill could not have known it, but my family's nickname for me was always 'Bunnie'.

CHEQUERS

We passed most weekends at Chequers, the old country house in Buckinghamshire kept for the Prime Minister's use. I slept in what is called the 'Prison Room'. So called, because Lady Mary Grey was said to have been imprisoned there by Queen Elizabeth I. She feared the Lady was about to force her claim to the throne. Going to bed on the first night, I saw the room had another door, but I was too tired to investigate. When I was dressing next morning, the butler, Sawyers, came in by the spare door to tell me Churchill demanded my presence. I found the door led to one of those mysterious private staircases that so often lead from one bedroom to another in the big old houses of England and France.

Chequers, with its enormous Great Hall, lit by stained-glass windows, gathered many great political and military leaders at the weekends. Mrs Hill or I would compile lists of the guests. One copy went to the guard commander, so he would know whom to admit. Another copy went to Mrs Churchill, who arranged the seating plans for lunch and dinner. She pointed out, it required great social knowledge and discretion to place the guests in the correct order around the table. She would consider giving each one the prestige of their rank. The highest would be the closest to Churchill. She also knew if there were any possible clashes of personality and avoided seating people together who did not get on. Though work did not slacken, I found the visits to Chequers a joy, because the maid brought me breakfast in bed. It was a real change from my dug-out room in the Annexe.

As the war went on, and the Allies suffered one set-back after another, Churchill became more engrossed in his work. His sense of humour faded by the day, and it was only with reluctance he gave time to relaxations - or even to meals. But there was one strange evening, during the days when we still managed to get down to Chartwell, when he relaxed in a way, that seemed out of character. Late one Saturday night, after dinner, he summoned me to his study. I went in and found him deep in conversation with Professor Lindeman, the great inventive genius known as 'The Prof', who had been his friend for many years. I sat behind the typewriter and waited. After a while, Churchill got up from his chair, put out most of the lights and switched on the radio. Then the two of them, ignoring my presence, sat listening to a dance band. I said nothing and crept away to bed when I thought they were not looking.

At Chequers, after dinner, Churchill would drift over to a bagatelle board which stood against a pillar in the Great Hall. While his visitors stood waiting for important conversations to begin, Churchill would play on the bagatelle board, alone, absorbed in the game and with care, totted up his score. Then he would put down the little cue and talk to his guests.

Tommy kept everyone out of the Great Hall if Churchill put on band music. I did not see it, but Churchill would march up and down for hours with tears flowing down his face if depressed. His favourite records, I could hear blaring out from the hall were, *Run Rabbit Run*, and

Keep Right On to the End of the Road, sung by the Scottish variety star, Sir Harry Lauder

Usually, his only relaxation was to watch an occasional film shown on home equipment. I remember Chaplin's, *The Great Dictator, Gone With the Wind, Lady Hamilton*, and Churchill's great favourites, the *Marx Brothers*. They seemed to have an invigorating effect on him, because he would jump up afterwards and say, "Come on, now we must do some work." I would be lucky to get to bed by 4 am.

It was during the showing of a Marx Brother film, Churchill learned of one of the war's most curious incidents. We were spending the weekend at Ditchley Park. We knew London was under its heaviest air attack so far, and Churchill had been in touch with the Home Security War Room, to learn of the extent of the damage. When he went into the hall to watch the film, I stayed by the telephone. A call came over the 'scrambler'. It was an urgent message for the Prime Minister. Rudolph Hess *(see note 5.),* a leading Nazi, had flown a plane to Britain and landed in Scotland.

It was normal procedure to type top secret messages and hand the paper to Churchill to read, so nobody would know what the message said, unless he chose to tell them. I typed the news about Hess. He had come on a one-man mission to try to arrange a separate peace between Britain and Germany. I called Churchill out of the hall and handed him the paper. I was not sure of the importance of Hess in the Nazi hierarchy but when I saw the Old Man's face, I realised something big had happened. He called a group of military chiefs out of the film show and took them to his office for a long discussion about what the news could mean.

After giving himself up, Hess had asked to speak to the Duke of Hamilton. The following day, the Duke met

48

with Hess, then came to Ditchley Park and gave a first-hand account of his meeting with the Nazi. The decision - Hess had no real influence with Adolf Hitler. He was imprisoned and later put on trial for crimes against humanity.

***

We were at Chequers when Churchill attempted to write a speech to stir the French people just before France capitulated in 1940.

"I propose to dictate in French," he announced. I wiped my hands - I felt anxious. His French, though knowledgeable, had a pronunciation which was all his own. For half an hour I tried to reproduce his words on the typewriter, but in the end, we gave it up. He said he would try again later, but we never did. I believe he got the help of a fluent French speaker to put the speech together. It was the famous speech when he offered joint citizenship between the British and the French nations - an offer - never taken up.

While at Chequers, Winston Churchill left there for his historic meeting with President Roosevelt at sea. This led to the Atlantic Charter. We all waited to see him leave, and he approached each of us in turn and gave us a farewell handshake.

Churchill was ready and raring to go early. He always liked to give the impression he waited for everybody else, but this was never so. Any departure usually meant the entire entourage hung around for anything from 10 minutes to two hours before he appeared. However long the wait, the result was invariably the same. The door would burst open, and Churchill, bustling through, would say, "We must be off now." No matter how long we had waited, he always managed to create the impression we were delaying him.

Of course - work held him back. He boasted he could bathe and dress in 13 minutes - though this was no great record when considering he had a valet on hand to run the bath and lay out his clothes. Certainly, for someone so heavily built, he could move fast.

Knowing his weakness about leaving on time, Mrs Churchill kept a keen eye on his movements, and I saw many examples of this while we were at Admiralty House. His bedroom and hers were joined by a door, and although the door was closed while he worked, Mrs Churchill never missed noticing when somebody came in to speak to him. During the break in dictation, she would whisper to me from her room, imploring me to remind her husband to bathe and dress in good time for dinner. She once told me an amusing story. He relied on her to keep him on time. They were going away for the weekend, and twice she reminded him of the hour. He continued to delay, and they arrived at the station to see their train drawing away. Churchill complained loud and clear, the train had 'left early'. His wife convinced him the train was on time - he was late. "But Clemmie," he said petulantly, "you only told me twice - you always tell me three times."

IT MUST BE LOVE

For a long time, Churchill shot me disapproving looks when he saw Tommy and I together. He knew Tommy was married, and although he would never dream of criticizing us, we could see the puzzled expression on his face as our friendship developed. Tommy found an opportunity to talk to him. He told the whole story, right back to the days when his late guard duties had caused the first rifts in his married life. Tommy pointed out on three separate occasions his superiors at Scotland Yard had asked for his return, and Churchill had protested, "No, Thompson. I'm the best judge of this. I want you near me. You understand me?"

Churchill listened for a long time as Tommy poured out his life story. And the Old Man, true to his nature, grew sentimental about the whole affair. The looks stopped.

***

We married in 1945, when it was clear the Allies would win the war. Without telling anyone, we slipped away to the Registry Office at Caxton Hall, a short walk away from the Prime Minister's home. I gave my address as 10, Downing Street, but the newspapers never noticed. Perhaps all the reporters were away at the war. Three months went by before anybody else knew we were man and wife. Churchill was not told until Tommy left his service after the war ended. The Old Man gave Tommy a cheque and said, "This will buy you a nice wedding present. I hope you will be very happy." He paused, then added, "You have married a very wonderful lady."

Mary Shearburn, Churchill's Secretary, or as we knew her, great Auntie May

We think Auntie May might have been asked to leave by Mrs Hill. Churchill disapproved of his secretary and his bodyguard becoming so close. Since Tommy was married (although going through a divorce), Churchill's senior staff did not want any scandal.

She left Churchill's service and went to work for the BBC. It seems she was there until the end of the war. Auntie May was a heavy smoker and she died a few months after Tommy, even though, only 15 years his junior.

10, Downing Street,
Whitehall.

To whom it may concern,

Miss Mary T.G. Shearburn has been a member
of my personal secretarial staff since April 1939.
She has a pleasant manner, and I have found her to be
willing and obliging, quick, intelligent, and an efficient
shorthand-typist.

Miss Shearburn now leaves me to take up another
post, and I wish her every success.

Winston S. Churchill

August 23, 1941.

Reference letter for Mary Shearburn from Churchill

10, Downing Street,
Whitehall.

I knew Miss M.T.G. Shearburn at 10 Downing Street from May 1940 to August 1941. As a shorthand-typist she is definitely in the first class — quick, accurate and willing, pleasant to work with and always completely unruffled.

J.M. Martin.
Principal Private
Secretary to the
Prime Minister

Reference letter from Churchill's Principal Secretary

To Tommy.

You brought me peace & comfort
    And a smile when my heart was sad.
You gave me your strength to lean on
    And my lonely heart was glad.

You gave me hope & courage
    And the joy of deep content.
You brought me love & companionship
    And all that your loving meant.

You gave me someone to turn to —
    Someone to call my own
And the sure & certain knowledge
    That I'm never more alone........

These things give life its meaning
    And make it fine & true...
So in return I bring my gift —
    My love, my sweet, to you!   Bunnie.
                                     3.12.44.

Letter to Tommy

55

WINSTON CHURCHILL.

"England! Awake!" - a voice cried, But we slept
And heeded not the voice of those who died,
That we might live,....the silent shadows crept
  Nearer and ever nearer to our side,
The war-machines of others did not sleep -
  Lulled by a sense of false security -
Their constant watch they dared not fail to keep
  Until their plans should reach maturity,
But we - in splendid blindness - did not hear
  The voice that would disturb our foolish peace.
The vision of one man - though crystal clear -
  Urged us to waken - urged and would not cease,...
Throughout the years of conflict he'd foretold
  He led us - faithfully and certainly,
Through the long night - when even hope grew cold
  He never failed us - surely, patiently,
He steered us through our country's darkest hour,
  Till the far-distant, shining goal was won,
And Britain, in her reborn strength and power
  Will not forget the courage of her son.
And we, whose lives and liberties we owe
  Must yet remember all that might have been
And yet may be if we should fail again
  To keep the course that he has made so plain.
All honour to the man whose steady hand
  Guided us through the turmoil and the strife
And drove the hordes from our beloved land
  Giving us freedom, hope reborn and life,
Aparing no effort in his ceaseless round
  Giving his every moment, thought and deed,
May we remember in our peace new found
  The man who never failed us in our need.

15. 5. 45

Poem by Mary Shearburn 1945

Mary and Walter on a speaking tour in their retirement

NOTES

1. Churchill's staff often referred to him affectionately, as 'The Old Man'.
2. Churchill had been informed by the Secret Service that Hitler's assassins were waiting for him at the Duke of Windsor's house.
3. This was Grace.
4. Tommy's son, Harold said his mother loved Tommy so much, she just wanted to see him happy. She loved him enough to let him go. It was not Mary Shearburn who wrecked Tommy's marriage. It was Churchill. Through all the years they were together, Churchill demanded Tommy be at his side every day and every night. In 1939 when Tommy went back to serve Churchill again, it was the end for Kate, his wife. Churchill ruined Tommy's private life and then seemed jealous he had struck up a friendship with Mary.
5. Hess was put in Spandau prison in Berlin for life. He died in1987 from a suspected suicide and the prison was demolished so it did not become a shrine for Nazis. He was 93.

Further Reading

This book is in a series of micro non- fiction books by Linda Stoker:

"Guard from the Yard"
"Churchill's Secretary"
"World War 2 Soldier" (coming Sept 2020)

Longer non-fiction:

"Churchill from the Fly on the Wall DET. INSP. Thompson"

Fiction based on truth:

"Churchill's Shadow"

Printed in Great Britain
by Amazon

78504467R00041